Firefighters

Julie Murray

Abdo
MY COMMUNITY: JOBS
Kids

abdopublishing.com

Published by Abdo Kids, a division of ABDO, PO Box 398166, Minneapolis, Minnesota 55439.
Copyright © 2016 by Abdo Consulting Group, Inc. International copyrights reserved in all countries.
No part of this book may be reproduced in any form without written permission from the publisher.

Printed in the United States of America, North Mankato, Minnesota.

052015

092015

THIS BOOK CONTAINS
RECYCLED MATERIALS

Photo Credits: Glow Images, iStock, Shutterstock © daseaford p.22, Taina Sohlman p.23 / Shutterstock.com

Production Contributors: Teddy Borth, Jennie Forsberg, Grace Hansen

Design Contributors: Candice Keimig, Dorothy Toth

Library of Congress Control Number: 2014958405

Cataloging-in-Publication Data

Murray, Julie.

 Firefighters / Julie Murray.

   p. cm. -- (My community: jobs)

ISBN 978-1-62970-913-0

Includes index.

1. Fire fighters--Juvenile literature. 2. Fire extinction--Staff--Juvenile literature. 3. Rescue work--Juvenile
literature.   I. Title.

628.9'25--dc23

2014958405

Table of Contents

Firefighters

Firefighters save lives.

They put out fires.

They get people to safety.

They help people who are hurt.

Carol was in a car accident.

They ride in a fire truck.

The siren is loud!

They hook up a hose.

Water sprays out.

13

They wear special clothes.

These keep them safe.

They need lots of tools.

Jim puts on his **air tank**.

Do you know a firefighter?

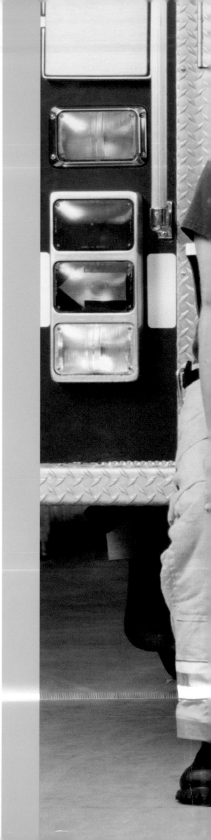

A Firefighter's Tools

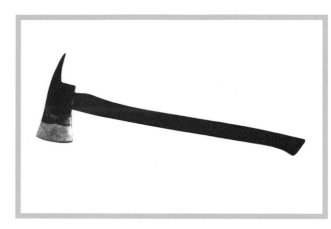

fire axe

fire hose

fire engine

helmet

Glossary

air tank
a compartment that holds air so firefighters can breathe while around smoke.

siren
a piece of equipment that makes a very loud warning sound.

Index

abdokids.com

Use this code to log on to abdokids.com and access crafts, games, videos, and more!

Abdo Kids Code:
MFK9130